SITUATIONS and LEADERSHIP

SHORT STORIES
AND
LIFELONG LESSONS

Ervin (Earl) Cobb
Charlotte D. Grant-Cobb, PhD

Ervin (Earl) Cobb and Charlotte D. Grant-Cobb, PhD
PRAISE FOR THEIR WORK

"There is nothing better than a good story. Utilizing very relevant stories that you can easily identify with tied to the highly actionable Skinny Principles makes for a great formula. A very useful and timely book for all professionals looking to advance their leadership skills."

— Barbara Cooper, CIO Toyota North America – Retired

"Charlotte and Earl are leaders and can teach leadership, a rare combination. The Smart Leader should hold a prominent place in your professional library."

— Jim Grigsby, President/CEO Jim Grigsby Consulting

"Master Teachers is my description of these authors. The Smart Leader is a must read for all leaders; especially for generations of future leaders."
— Selma C. Dean, ED.D. , Pastoral and Community Counselor, Educator, Inspirational Speaker

"Written from practical experience and success. An inspiration!"
— Robert Bunnett, Chief Operating Officer, LSI

"Earl Cobb has done it again with his new book. Earl is that rarest of authors. He writes with the power of someone who has been there."
— Doug Russell, Marketing Director, SmartPro Financial

"Mr. Cobb has captured the pure essence of Leadership in this work. His broad-based experience guides his insight in every topical area."
— Albert L. McHenry, Ph.D., Emeritus Faculty, Arizona State University

"Busy leaders need practical guidance and an easy-to-follow format which is what this book provides. The authors have culled their years of experience and in a story format. By doing so, they have provided a path for leaders to follow. I hope others may benefit from their expertise and apply the "Skinny" Principles to their respective paths. Kudos!"
— Dr. G. Mick Smith, Executive Regional Director, Challenger School Foundation

Ervin (Earl) Cobb and Charlotte D. Grant-Cobb, PhD
PRAISE FOR THEIR WORK

"As major transitions in the world are transpiring, leadership requires a broader and deeper understanding of today's organizations and the individuals that lead them. The SMART Leader and the "Skinny" Principles proffers that leaders are expected to act and think differently, not just to survive, but to thrive in this changing organizational landscape."

— Rufus Glasper, Ph.D., President and CEO, League for Innovation, Chancellor Emeritus, Maricopa Community Colleges

"Mr. Cobb has been meticulously working on advancing what is known in the realm of Leadership Development. He is a proven author of several books, a well-known speaker, a leader, and has a genius approach to leadership development. The information that he provides in his latest body of work is "textbook worthy" and I highly recommend all colleges/universities/companies adopt this body of work to teach Leadership Development"

— Jonathan Hebert, M. Eng, PMP, Ph.D., Program

"The Cobbs have written a leadership book that is easy to read with practical, apply it right now, techniques. This book is chock full of tips, techniques, and best practices in leadership that will be of value to new leaders of any generation. Their "Skinny" Principles, shared in each chapter, will undoubtedly be earmarked and highlighted by readers and referred to regularly. This book is a MUST READ for new leaders. Plus, leaders who have been in their role for a while will likely also find a nugget or two to take away and apply."

— Gina Abudi, MBA, President, Abudi Consulting Group, LLC, Author of *Implementing Positive Organizational Change: A Strategic Project Management Approach*, J Ross Publishing, 2017

OTHER BOOKS BY

Ervin (Earl) Cobb and Charlotte D. Grant-Cobb, PhD

Leadership Front and Center
A Decade of Thought and Tutelage

The SMART Leader and the Skinny Principles
How to Win and Lead within Any Organization

Driving Ultimate Project Performance
Transforming from Project Manager to Project Leader

**The Official Leadership Checklist and Diary
for Project Management Professionals**

The Leadership Advantage
Do More. Lead More. Earn More.

God's Goodness & Our Mindfulness
Responding versus Reacting to Life Changing Circumstances

Focused Leadership
What You Can Do Today To Become a More Effective Leader

Transition
Solace and Comfort for the Broken Hearted

Pillow Talk Consciousness
Intimate Reflections on America's 100 Most Interesting
Thoughts and Suspicions

Navigating the Life Enrichment Model™

Living a Richer Life
Getting the Most out of Life's Gifts and Circumstances

Until I Change
Affirmations for Mastering Personal Change

DEDICATION

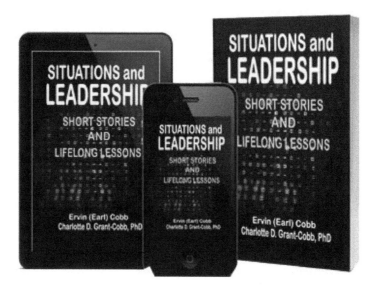

We dedicate this book to you, the reader.

We applaud your desire to learn more about how the most important personal and professional situations we all face every day can significantly impact our lives and our success.

We believe that by being willing to strengthen the primary set of leadership skills you need to effectively respond to the challenging situations in your life, you will reap the personal, professional and financial rewards that accompany proactively improving critical thinking skills and being prepared.

Published by RICHER Press
An Imprint of Richer Life, LLC
5710 Ogeechee Road, Suite 200-175, Savannah, Georgia 31405
www.richerlifellc.com

Cover Design: RICHER Media USA
Photographs: Bigstock

The stories included are a work of fiction. Names, characters, places and incidents are the product of the author's imagination or are used fictitiously. Any resemblance to actual persons, living or dead, events or locales is entirely coincidental.

Volume book discounts are available for groups, companies and organizations. Contact the publisher for information and order instructions.

Library of Congress Control Number: 2020949992

Situations and Leadership
Short Stories and Lifelong Lessons

Ervin (Earl) Cobb and Charlotte D. Grant-Cobb, PhD

1. Leadership   2. Management   3. Self-Improvement
(pbk : alk. Paper)

ISBN: 978-1-7335693-1-6

PRINTED IN THE UNITED STATES OF AMERICA

eBook Version - January 2021
Paperback Version - February 2021

CONTENTS

INTRODUCTION

 We think that you will agree that most of our professional and personal lives are crammed with challenging situations. Many of these situations and related circumstances can and often generate negative consequences and outcomes. Certain outcomes can negatively shape the trajectory of our careers, the richness of our lives and even cause lifelong regret.

Fortunately, in countless cases, life gives us a second chance. A second chance to get it right or make it better. Fully taking advantage of these second chances depends on which of the following segments of the population you choose to join.

1. Some people prepare for the next time a similar or new situation surfaces by learning from their prior experiences or the experiences of others. They also find themselves enjoying the rewards of self-improvement and mastering the art of personal and professional resiliency.

2. Others are aware of the likelihood of a second chance yet find themselves surprised and unprepared when they do come face-to-face with a similar or new situation. They can only hope for the best and accept disappointing outcomes.

3. While most people don't even recognize that a second chance or an even more difficult situation is just around the corner. When the situation surfaces, they tend to believe that it is just their fate to have such a "problem" and hope all goes well.

In our most recent research and studies, we have found that the most common and challenging situations we all face in life are situations involving *organizational relationships* with others. By organizational relationships, we are referring to relationships built around the acceptance of common goals, the existence of levels of hierarchy and the need for timely and quality decisions.

11

We also have found that one of the things commonly lacking for most of us (*and naturally pushes us into segment 2 or 3*) is the lack of effective leadership skills. That is to say, the distinctive set of skills required in the intellectually driven process of evaluating, understanding and responding to these challenging situations.

With so much involved in organizational interactions of any type, why do effective "leadership skills" play such a key role in this process? The quick answer here is two-fold.

Firstly, we must accept the reality that just as taking the next breath or speaking the next sentence "leadership" is *embedded* within all verbal interactions which require a decision to be made. At a minimum, "leadership" in these situations encompasses the following: understanding each situation; being cognizant of with whom you are speaking; evaluating the possible responses to the next question (*before it comes out of your mouth*); maintaining the best tone of voice; providing the best rationale to support your own position and deciding how to fittingly finish the conversation. All of this must be done during each interaction and in real-time.

Secondly, even though each situation will be unique, effective leadership skills, your experience and your lessons learned will allow you quickly see what's on the horizon and help you frame the best way to handle the situation at hand.

In *"Situations and Leadership"*, we have carefully created ten short, color-illustrated and suspenseful stories for you to enjoy and to help you *"walk in the shoes"* of the protagonists. Each story represents a unique real-life situation. The stories entertainingly unpack important leadership lessons. The questions at the end of each story and your self-analysis of each situation will strengthen your skills and vicariously enhance your preparation to generate more positive and rewarding outcomes. We believe the lessons you learn will improve your mastery of essential leadership skills, help you take full advantage of all chances to effectively lead in challenging situations and strengthen your overall resiliency.

CHAPTER ONE

NO, MY DEAR. YOU HAVE A LEADERSHIP DILEMMA

My name is Marilynn Renee Mason-Taylor. I have always been a focused, hardworking and manager. I have both a BA and MBA.

However, I currently feel incredibly lonely, defeated and like a real loser.

Here's why.

Over the past fifteen years, I have worked my way up the ranks of a major federal government Agency. Three years ago, I was promoted to the grade of GS-14. A year ago, I was selected over ten other candidates to lead the organization and new function within the same Agency.

Unlike any of the organizations I have managed in the past, more than eighty percent of my new team is under thirty-five years of age. Half of them work predominantly from home. Most of my team members are also new to this Agency and have a lot to learn about the new operational processes and goals of the new function.

But, with my wealth of management experience at various levels within this Agency, I felt that I could teach them how the "old guys" do it and give them a "leg up" compared to their co-workers in other organizations. In addition, since I was at least 10 years older than most of them, I assumed that they would easily listen to me and follow my carefully worded directions.

When I accepted this position, the idea of creating and leading a new Agency organization and functional operation appeared to be a great opportunity. I was looking forward to reaching the enviable, GS-15 grade in short order.

Well, the past twelve months have been the worst period in my entire career. My health is failing. My manager has less time to spend with me. My co-workers are not as talkative when I am around them these days and I find it difficult to get up and come in to work. Over the last few weeks, I have been waking up concerned that I would soon be replaced or even dismissed, and my career would be in shambles.

Here is some of what has occurred since I took over the new organization and why I now feel so defeated.

- Three months into my new management role, I was drowning in internal meetings and conference calls involving almost every member of my team. There were so many calls and so many questions that I had to institute a policy that would limit our team meetings to one forty-five-minute gathering per week. All conference calls must now have to be approved, at least a week in advance. I was also forced to change my office "open door" policy from anytime to only two hours a day on Wednesdays and Fridays.

- Limiting the communications with and between my team members did have the effect of slowing down what I thought were unproductive meetings and calls. However, within a few months, more and more team members began to miss important deadlines. I found myself having to meet with each one of them individually to ensure that everyone knew what I expected. I used the time to let them know that I was not pleased with their job performance and I knew that they could do better. I also made sure they knew what I would not tolerate.

- Last fall, I was forced to cancel the annual Team Holiday Party. Through the grapevine, I found out that many of my team members were spending time with managers in other Agency organizations chatting and complaining about how my department's operational processes didn't allow them to make real time decisions that would reduce inefficiencies and complete more work in less time. Yet not even one of my team members bothered to bring any of these suggestions to my attention.

I feel that things really began to go downhill a few weeks ago. I learned that when I missed the first half a quarterly meeting with my co-workers and our Agency's top executives that much of that time was spent discussing how poorly my organization was functioning. Also, my peers shared that they were concerned about how my team is not  working productively with the other teams within the Agency.

Last week, I accidentally ran into an old friend and mentor who I have known since graduate school. Over coffee, I shared with him my current management dilemma.

He sat quietly for a while and finally said, "No, my dear. You have a leadership dilemma." Then, he asked me three questions that I could not answer affirmatively, and that I will never forget:

1. *"When you accepted the position, did you consider what leadership skills you would need to successfully lead a new organization?"*

2. *"Have you had any training in what it takes and how to lead millennials?"*

3. *"It sounds like to me that your actions and thinking are those of a manager and not a leader. Are you aware of the difference between managing and leading?"*

I must admit that I did take a few courses in graduate school where we discussed leadership styles and common leadership traits. However, I never took any of that stuff seriously.

Leadership versus Management...does it really matter?

Questions to Ponder

1. How would you describe Marilynn's situation?

2. Do you believe that Marilynn moved into her new position overconfident and for the wrong reasons?

   Why or why not?

3. If you are ten years older than the team members you manage, what are some of the things you should consider ?

   Why?

4. When should Marilynn have first noticed the situation she was in and what should she have done differently at that point?

5. Why was taking the step to limit communications with and among her team not a good idea?

6. Should Marilynn have proactively reached out for professional coaching or counsel instead of waiting a year and accidently running into someone who she could trust?

   Why or why not?

7. What is the major difference between managing and leading and why the outcome of many situations depends on which role you choose during your interactions with others.

What are some of the lessons you should take away from this story and situation?

1. Understanding the difference between management and leadership and choosing the proper role to take on during interactions with others will significantly impact the outcome of most challenging situations.
2.
3.
4.
5.
6.
7.
8.

CHAPTER TWO

I THOUGHT THEY REALLY KNEW ME

It was around 12:45 PM on Wednesday afternoon and Mark Ashford has just returned from lunch. He intentionally returned a little early so that he could find a seat at the table near the rear of the large conference room.

Today is the big day. This afternoon he will finally receive the anxiously anticipated *"letters from home"*. This confidential feedback will give Mark a deeper appreciation of how his managers, a few co-workers and some subordinates perceive his leadership skills and behaviors. It should confirm his perception of how his organization views his leadership ability and set the stage for his elevation to vice president.

Mark was one of forty-five managers from companies located throughout the United States and Canada attending the five-day,

19

internationally admired Senior Leadership Development Program (SLDP) offered by the Creative Leadership Academy.

Mark was not surprised his manager, Jack Kerry, selected him to attend this type of prestigious development program. He joined Medco Technologies ten years ago as a Senior Project Manager.

He had just added a PMP certification to his academic credentials, which include an engineering degree and an MBA. Mark was promoted a year ago to the role of the company's Corporate Manager of Project Management. Historically, the position has been a stepping-stone for being elevated to vice president. The recent promotion gave Mark the opportunity, for the first time, to lead a functional organization within Medco and to spend time with other department managers.

Due to the total cost of this pristine leadership development program, including the travel from Chicago to San Diego, it required the approval of the company's President, Durrell Billis.

Both Jack and Mr. Billis had attended the SLDP earlier in their careers and thought that it was one of the best programs of its type in North America. They valued the SLDP's intensity and the assessment tools used to help participants individually grasp important insights regarding their current leadership skills, behaviors and shortcomings based on anonymous feedback from key members within their organizations.

One unique aspect of the SLDP is the team of carefully chosen career psychologist brought in to spend four full hours with each participant on the fourth day of the Program.

The timing was important because on the third day of the Program, the training facilitator would provide each participant the results and feedback from a 360-degree Leadership Assessment. Each Program participant is required to complete and return the fully completed assessment package at least 30 days prior to the start of the Program.

Shortly after 1:15 PM, the big conference room was now full of participants and the Program facilitator entered the room with a stack of thick envelopes. The third day of the Program was always on a Wednesday and had become known as *"reality check Wednesday"*. The feedback from the 360-degree Leadership Assessment was jokingly referred to as the *"letters from home"*.

There were stories of how some past SLDP participants were so surprised by the feedback from their organization that they left the Program before the Friday close. Some even suffered nervous breakdowns and others later unexpectedly left their companies and management careers prematurely.

However, Mark was confident that he would get good results and positive feedback. He felt he was a natural leader. The reason he wanted a seat near the rear of the room this afternoon was to watch the reactions on the faces of other participants as they opened their *"letters from home"*.

As the SLDP facilitator approached his seat, Mark noticed that the expression on her face was one of concern. As he opened his envelope, he went straight to the anonymous feedback sections at the end of the purposefully arranged package.

The feedback was separated into three categories labeled: *"From Your Management"*, *"From Your Co-workers"* and *"From Your Subordinates"*. On the cover page of each category was a scoring bar, which ranged from 10% to 100%, representing the percentile of positive responses based on the Program's 23-year history of ranking Program participant feedback. Participants whose ranking were less than 50% were considered at risk and in need of significant improvement in their leadership skills and behaviors.

To Mark's bewilderment, he noticed that his ranking for each feedback category was less than 50%. As he slowly sank down into his chair, he said to himself, *"I thought they really knew me"*.

Tonight, he would be required to agonizingly read the complete assessment and disappointing feedback from his organization. He left the conference room that afternoon wondering what had gone wrong. He wondered what he would say to the career psychologist that he was scheduled to spend time with on Thursday afternoon.

After a long and sleepless night of tossing and turning, Mark walked into a small meeting room Thursday afternoon where he

found a middle-aged man named Joel Collins waiting. Joel was the career psychologist that had been assigned to work with Mark. Joel introduced himself and indicated that he had thoroughly reviewed Mark's assessment results and feedback. Joel suggested that they start their time together by having Mark respond to a few leadership patterns and behaviors that he had identified while analyzing the feedback from Mark's managers, co-workers and subordinates. Mark agreed and said in a dejected voice, *"Joel, I must admit that I am extremely disappointed. I thought they really knew me"*.

Joel gently responded with, *"I know you are disappointed Mark. But, based on my professional analysis of all your assessment results as well as the level of detail in your feedback, I believe that, as a leader, they may know you better than you know yourself."*

Then, Joel initiated their counseling and coaching session with the following set of questions. Understandably, Mark's responses were somewhat emotional. Nevertheless, he was determined to respond to each question as honest and truthful as possible.

Joel: *Since you moved into your current "functional" management role from your "matrixed" project management role, have you felt a need to adjust your leadership approach?*

Mark: No. I was a successful Project Manager. All my current managers know my reputation and what I have done in the past. What I did to successfully lead my project teams as a Project Manager is what I plan to do in my new role — given enough time.

Joel: *Okay. It looks like you have been in your new position for about a year now. Have you been as successful in your new role as Corporate Manager of Project Management as you were in your prior position?*

Mark: Well, I must admit that the first six months or so were a little rocky and some things have gone wrong. However, I am sure that Jack and Mr. Billis understand that it will take a while for me to get up the learning curve. However, I do feel that I have done a decent job so far. They should have given me a break in their feedback.

Joel: *Okay. Have you met with all your current direct reports to learn what they think about you and the direction you are taking the organization? Have you taken the time to share with your entire team "who you are" and what they should expect from you as their new leader?*

Mark: No. Not yet. However, it's on my list. Nevertheless, my new team should realize that it will take time for them to get use to me and my leadership style. I have not had a chance to do any of those things. But I will get around to it.

Joel spent the remainder of their time together walking Mark through all the assessment results. He also took the time to give Mark his professional opinions on the numerous comments included in the Assessment feedback from his managers, co-workers, and subordinates.

After about three and a half hours, Mark began to realize that Joel was correct. Based on *what he had done* to date and the *actions* and *inaction* his organization had witnessed since he accepted the new leadership role, *"they did know him better than he knew himself."*

Questions to Ponder

1. How would you describe Mark's situation?

2. Why do you think Mark was so confident that he would get good results and positive feedback on his leadership assessment?

3. What do you think you would say to a psychologist if you found yourself in this situation?

4. It appears that Mark assumed his organization's management and team members would provide positive feedback because of his past recognition as a "successful Project Manager."

   How did this assumption contribute to Mark's situation.

5. If you move into a new role or position, do you believe that your new team members should "realize that it will take time for them to get use to you" and how you deal with challenging situations?

   Why or who not?

6. Should "what you have done in the past" automatically give people the confidence that you will do as well in a different role or different situation?

7. Based on this story, when facing a new or unfamiliar situation, what are the most important things you should keep in mind?

What are some of the lessons you should take away from this story and situation?

1. In all situations, my level of influence, control and success will be based upon how others in the situation perceive me as a leader and the actions I take in the moment.
2.
3.
4.
5.
6.
7.
8.

CHAPTER THREE

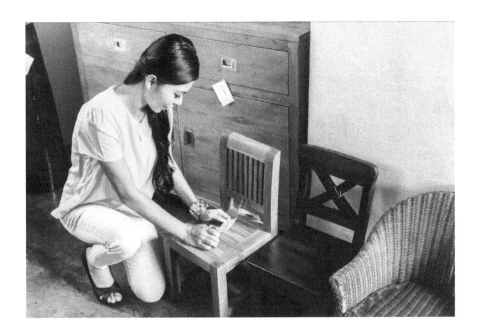

I WAS BORN TO DO THIS

My Dad loved reproducing antique furniture and he started our family business in his woodworking shop. When the "naked oak" craze was all the rage in the 1970's, Dad took the family savings and invested in unfinished "naked oak" furniture.

It didn't take long for my Dad, Julius Lee, to realize that people loved the idea of doing it themselves. Therefore, once they saw Dad's pieces, they were happy to purchase the furniture kits and thrilled about the idea of DIY.

As the retail part of the business expanded, Dad cut back on his own woodworking and hired four full time furniture makers and two apprentices for the shop. Soon, over fifty percent of Lee's Fine Custom Furnishings retail sales were custom antique reproduction kits. The remaining sales were from our custom, "unfinished" line. The "naked oak" phase eventually died off, but customers kept returning to say hello, browse and purchase our customized furniture and furniture kits.

A few years later, Dad invested in a large warehouse and storefront. It was on a corner lot located on North Hayden Road and Thomas in Old Town Scottsdale, Arizona — where it stands today.

Dad started scanning the country, contracting with other artisans to add uniquely designed furniture and accessories to the store's growing inventory.

I'm CeCe Lee and from the time I saw my first antique reproduction, I knew my life would always involve art and furniture.

At the age of twelve, I was sketching furniture designs and sourcing pieces for the store. When I entered my teens, Dad let me pick several new pieces of furniture. Most never sold, like the turtle coffee table and pelican lamp. After two years on the floor, Dad just removed the price tags from those two pieces and made them our store "mascots."

They later became a running joke between the staff and me.

Art and history are in my blood, so naturally I majored in art history in college. While in college, I thoroughly enjoyed the campus life. However, I missed my daily visits to the store and being in the comfort of the retail environment. I would go into the store while on college breaks and the salesclerks would always rib me with a greeting, "CeCe, I almost sold the turtle coffee table today!"

I have always considered myself a part of the Lee's Fine Custom Furnishings family. However, it was a big surprise when Dad offered me a job. Initially, I thought he was just being generous.

He certainly didn't have to put me on the payroll. After all, I started contributing my designs when I was twelve and I was continuing to be an active part of the design team.

Then, Dad added, *"I think it's time for me to start grooming you to one-day take a leadership role in the business."* This was even a bigger surprise. I did believe that I was becoming an incredibly good designer, but I never felt that I would be particularly good at running the business.

By 2000, seventy percent of Lee's Fine Custom Furnishings sales revenue came from our own customized design and antique reproduction furniture lines. A larger percentage of the orders were now requiring shipping across the country. Fortunately, Dad was exceptionally good at managing production and packaging costs. Therefore, even when sales required shipping, Lee's retail prices, including shipping cost, were always competitive.

In 2001, Lee's Fine Custom Furnishings published its first product and sales catalog. The catalog was easily adapted to what is now Lee's online presence. Like almost everything related to the real estate and housing market between 2006 and 2009, Lee's business was critically impacted by the Great Recession. Lee's survived the crash and stayed afloat. It was all due to my Dad's ability to minimize inventory levels, control raw materials cost and obtain short-term financing to support cash flow.

Our core staff stayed with us through the "crash" and by 2014, Lee's sales revenue was on an upswing. Dad was able to add a full-time designer, a sales manager and two part-time retail salesclerks. He also developed a contract relationship with a retail marketing firm to update the store sales and marketing strategy.

Just after Dad watched me graduate with my PhD in Art History from the University of Arizona, he told me he was thinking about selling the business. I almost fell off my Wegner reproduction.

I hated the thought of selling our family business. I guess I thought Lee's would go on forever. Dad shared that the only option to not selling would be for me to take over the business. I said, *"Dad, I love Lee's. But surely you know my designer's eye would not be enough to run our family business."*

Dad just smiled and said, *"CeCe, you were born to do this."*

It did seem to be the perfect time for me to take over Lee's Fine Custom Furnishings. The new home and construction industry were growing again, and our customer base was expanding. However, in the past, while spending much of my life in the store, I just couldn't seem to figure out the business side of things.

After some serious consideration, I told Dad I would give it a try. Therefore, after all the years of working around the business, I started my first official apprenticeship — to learn how to be successful at running the business.

My Dad just hung back for the first few weeks, allowing me to "get the feel" for the job. I had no problem getting acquainted with the market strategy and big picture of the furniture business. I also quickly began to understand each of the many moving parts of the business operations. However, figuring out how to make them work together to become a successful enterprise became more and more challenging. As I began to get more involved in day-to-day activities, I was beginning to really lose confidence in what I was doing. I also began to seriously doubt if I could really do this.

From a distance, Dad made it all look easy. But, after only a few months, I was ready to quickly return to teaching and designing. However, the thought of a future without Lee's Fine Custom Furnishings was even more frightening.

Feeling a little frustrated and confused, I went to Dad with the "white towel" in hand.

Dad said, *"CeCe. It takes time to learn how to make it all work. I'm glad it looked like it was easy, but it was just experience and some key time management skills. Let's try something different."*

For the next six months, I worked closely with Dad. I shadowed him as he went about managing and leading every aspect of the business. I watched him as he managed the retail operations, attracted new customers, gained repeat business, controlled inventory, managed cash flow and kept the entire staff motivated.

The most time-consuming efforts appeared to be associated with how Dad masterfully interfaced with the material wholesalers and how he was able to connect with the mostly remote team members handling online customer orders.

One night at dinner, I said to him, *"Dad, it's amazing to see how you seem to always be in the right place at just the right time."*

My Dad replied, *"Yes, my dear, that does appear to be one of my best acts."*

After about a year and a half, I was fully in charge of all business operations. Two years after that, my Dad officially retired and I finally became the new owner and leader of Lee's Fine Custom Furnishings. Over the next five years, there were some ups and

31

downs, but the business grew at a manageable rate and was profitable.

While shadowing my Dad and learning the "skinny" of how to run a small business, I learned some key and incredibly important lessons from him — such as how to be a "good manager" and how to balance the "ebb and flow" of a retail sales organization.

My Dad's gift of providing sound advice also continued to be amazing. There is one special piece of advice that I received from him regarding my responsibility as both a business owner and a "good leader" that I will never forget.

The special piece of advice was for me to remember that, as a leader, *"where you spend your time is not your choice, it's your responsibility."*

Thanks to my amazing Dad and his trust in me, I now realize that *"I was born to do this"*.

Questions to Ponder

1. How would you describe CeCe's situation?

2. Why do you think CeCe was hesitant to join her father in the family business?

3. It appeared to CeCe that her father made it all look easy. Have you ever found yourself in a situation where something was hard for you, yet it appeared easy for others.

   What did you do and why?

4. Is it possible to *"always be in the right place at just the right time"* in all situations.?

   Why or why not?

5. Why is it important to manage your time such that you are available when a challenging situation needs your immediate involvement?

6. What does *"where you spend your time is not your choice, it's your responsibility"* mean to you?

What are some of the lessons you should take away from
this story and situation?

1.	To help shape the best outcome in challenging situations, I must make sure that my involvement is substantive, timely and consistent with my level of responsibility.
2.	
3.	
4.	
5.	
6.	
7.	
8.	

CHAPTER FOUR

I SIMPLY PLAYED THE CARDS I WAS DEALT

My name is Sara Hornbill, and I am the CEO of a multi-national specialty products company. With over 1,500 retail sales locations throughout the Americas, Canada and most of the European Union, Walbash International, operates on narrow profit margins. We have hundreds of direct competitors who are constantly seeking to take market share.

For us, the key to staying financially afloat in any region is the ability of each location's General Manager to negotiate a reduced wholesale purchase cost for our products and to win competitive bids on mega-quantities of bestselling products and top brands.

35

I consider myself an empathetic leader, but rarely do I ask any of my General Managers to visit me in our corporate office in New York City and take the time out of their busy schedules to share with me how they orchestrated a big win or a suffered a big lost.

However, I considered this unique situation worthy of such an unusual request. I invited Alex Vanberry to join me in my office a few weeks ago for a postmortem review on how he and his Portugal-based team were able to successfully negotiate one of the largest mega-quantity wins and business turnarounds in our company's fifteen-year history.

Alex joined Walbash International four years ago with proven management skills but with only a few years of global retail sales experience.

When he accepted the General Manager's role in Lisbon last year, the location was operating at a financial lost and needed to quickly revamp its product line and win new market share to survive.

This could only be achieved by winning competitive bids for new name brand products that were available and selling like hotcakes throughout the EU.

Due to budget constraints, Alex was only allowed to take with him to Lisbon a couple of senior retail professionals he had known in his previous assignments. Thus, with this limitation, he would have to utilize the existing staff to achieve some challenging goals and to prevent Walbash International from shutting down the location.

When Alex walked into my New York office for our meeting, I had four questions prepared to ask and to probe into his recent accomplishments.

My questions were based on my keen knowledge of the situation and work environment he walked into when he accepted the Lisbon job. I thought that by asking him this set of specific questions, we could cut to the chase. My goal was to quickly gain an understanding of whether this *amazing feat* could be replicated in other Walbash International locations.

The first question I asked Alex was:

What did you perceive as your top challenge in your new role doing the first few weeks on the job?

Alex's reply was:

"Well, since I was going into a situation with only two team members that I was familiar with, I quickly realized that I was technically the new guy on the block.

Therefore, I perceived my top challenge as the need to become familiar with the team members I inherited and who had to do the work required for us to achieve the company goals. I spent most of my time the first few weeks getting to know each of my team members. I wanted to know their strengths, their weaknesses, their fears and what they needed from me to be successful.

I felt that if I could put myself in their shoes, I would be able to understand the cards I had to play, if you will, to have a chance to turn things around and get some much-needed wins."

The second question I asked was:

How did you determine what your primary role should be as the leader of an organization burdened with such financial and organizational challenges?

Alex's reply was:

"That was easy. Once I determined that the staff I had inherited was an experienced team, I spent the time to listen to them. Their assessment of our current business challenges was quite insightful. Then, when I learned that they were well schooled in negotiating with the local product wholesaler community and familiar the new products we needed to revamp the product line, I just had to make sure of two things. First, I had to ensure the entire team understood my turn-around strategy. Secondly, I had to clearly share with them what I expected from each of them and what I was willing to do to help them be successful."

The third question I asked was:

In your opinion, what was missing in the organization when you arrived and how may it have contributed to the organization's poor performance?

Alex's reply was:

In my opinion, what was sorely missing was an adequate level of senior leadership presence. By this I mean, someone who understood and accepted the fact that his or her job was <u>not</u> to <u>do</u> <u>the</u> <u>work</u>, but to understand the capabilities of each team member and to make sure that they "all" were in the best position to win and deliver the results needed.

The final question I asked Alex was:

In a few words, how would you summarize the approach you used to lead your team to such a high level of success?

Alex's reply was:

"Well, with limited staffing options and mounting challenges, I was forced to be a leader and not just a manager. I quickly recognized that winning within an organizational structure is indeed a team sport.

Organizationally, I needed them, and they needed me.

38

Therefore, I committed the time to get to know each team member's capabilities, strengths, and weaknesses as well as the role I needed to play to get the most out of each member's contribution to achieving our goals.

From there, as the game of winning bids for key products and successfully increasing product sales unfolded, I simply played the cards I was dealt"

In hindsight, what I gained from my postmortem review with Alex Vanberry was a decisive affirmation of the fact that the fundamentals of what it takes to be an effective leader and to get consistently outstanding organizational results are rather basic.

However, a manager's ability to recognize the significant value of these leadership fundamentals and to effectively apply and benefit from them is the true leadership challenge.

I was also reminded of how difficult a task it would be for me to replicate Alex's *amazing feat* without having more leaders like Alex in the organization.

Questions to Ponder

1. How would you describe Sara's situation?

2. How would you describe Alex's situation?

3. Why do you think the first thing Alex did in his situation was to get to know the associates on his new team?

4. Why was it smart of Alex to be interested in the capabilities of each of his team members to help develop a solution to the situation he inherited.?

5. What did Alex understand about his role as the leader and his responsibility to turn around the situation?

6. What techniques and exercises can you do to better understand the capabilities, strengths, and weaknesses in others prior to getting involved in challenging situations?

7. Name some of the ways you would "connect the dots" between other's capabilities and the objective you need to achieve.

What are some of the lessons you should take away from this story and situation?

1. To achieve the best results during challenging situations, I should take the time to understand the strengths and capabilities of others involved. The goal should be to construct a solution, which embraces these strengths and capabilities.
2.
3.
4.
5.
6.
7.
8.

"Whether pleasure or pain; every situation in your life serves a purpose. It is up to us to recognize what that purpose could be."

~ Dr. Steve Maraboli

Dr. Steve Maraboli is a life-changing Speaker, bestselling Author, and Behavioral Science Academic. His empowering and insightful words have been shared and published throughout the world in more than 25 languages.

CHAPTER FIVE

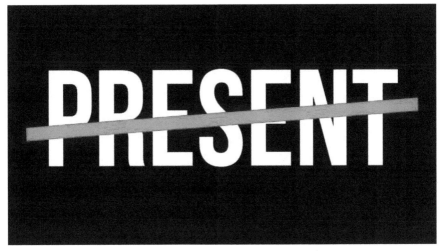

AN ASTONISHING LACK OF
LEADERSHIP PRESENCE

My long flight arrived in Charlotte, North Carolina at approximately eleven o'clock Thursday night. The flight from Phoenix was over four hours and fortunately, it was without any delays. It was after  midnight by the time I collected my bag, caught a cab and checked into my downtown hotel room.

My wife and I lived in the Charlotte area for about seven years in the early 2000s. I was quite familiar with Charlotte's downtown development history and was eager to see what had changed over the past decade. However, there will not be any time this trip for a tour of the Queen City to satisfy my curiosity.

43

This is an unscheduled and unusual business trip and mission for me. This business trip only permits me to spend twenty-four hours here in Charlotte. My mission is to conduct a corporate investigation and to prepare a confidential report this weekend in support of a Monday morning deliverable commitment I made to a special client earlier this week.

My first meeting will start at seven in the morning and I will most likely not complete all my meetings and interviews until late in the evening. Why am I here, you ask? First, let me take the time to share with you a little background on myself and some basic, but important, insights into the disturbing, yet often repeated, organizational performance challenge I have been asked to investigate.

****

My name is Anthony Jerome McAdoo. Most people call me AJ.

I retired from my 30-year career in corporate America around ten years ago. My last corporate position was as a Senior Technology Manager and the Head of Data Center Management for the Capital Cargo Bank.

On Monday of this week, I attended an Executive Leadership Conference in San Francisco. While there, I met Ralph Dean, the new President and CEO of the Capital Cargo Bank. He moved into this role after I had left Capital Cargo in 2009. During a lunch conversation, I shared with Ralph a few highlights of my tenure with Capital Cargo. I also mentioned the fact that I was attending this special leadership conference because I am now an organizational leadership development consultant with a keen interest in helping leaders understand the true power of leadership.

I was somewhat surprised when Ralph asked if I could meet him for dinner that same evening. He wanted to discuss a somewhat mystifying organizational and business performance challenge he and the Capital Cargo executive team were currently facing. Not satisfied with the feedback he was receiving from a consultant he hired a few months ago, he indicated that he was interested in getting another perspective on the challenge. I said, *"Sure. It would be my pleasure."*

I met Ralph for dinner that evening around eight-thirty. I must admit that I was a little shocked with his degree of candor. I learned that he was genuinely concerned about a presentation he had to give to Capital Cargo Bank's Board of Directors in a meeting scheduled for next week.

It turns out that Capital Cargo has experienced multiple outages of their online banking system over the past six months. All the outages were traced back to a critical Data Center located in Charlotte, North Carolina.

The daylong outages were having a severely negative impact on Capital Cargo's customer base and stock price. Any additional outages simply could not be tolerated.

Surprisingly, after several weeks of working with a consultant who was dispatched to Charlotte to determine the root cause of the problem, Ralph's executive team still could not provide him an explanation of the problem that he felt was adequate. In his words, *"The explanations I have been given to this point simply don't hold water; and can't be presented to my Board of Directors next Tuesday."*

After providing an hour-long breakdown of the situation and the most recent findings, Ralph asked if I could take a trip to the Charlotte Data Center and spend a day with the Data Center senior management team. He also asked if I would provide him a report detailing what I thought was the root cause of the problems and what might be a possible solution. He needed the report the following Monday.

Having a technical background, Ralph was less concerned with the feedback he had received regarding the technical issues and more concerned with what he perceived in his words, as *"a lack of senior leadership focus and organizational cohesiveness"*.

Sensing that Ralph was sincerely interested in getting my perspective and that he would give my report a fair hearing, I agreed to modify my schedule to include a trip to Charlotte later in the week. The plan will be to learn about the root cause of Capital Cargo's situation and determine a possible solution.

****

Thus, here I am in Charlotte. As I mentioned earlier, tomorrow I will meet with the Charlotte Data Center management team. I also plan to meet with and interview as many of the members of the Charlotte work team as  possible. My goal is to gain some operative insight into what is really happening at Capital Cargo's Charlotte Center, both operationally and organizationally. I intend to provide a report to Ralph Dean on Monday morning.

****

Well, it's early Saturday morning and I am back in my office in Phoenix working to complete the report I will deliver to Ralph Dean and Capital Cargo Monday morning. For about three hours now, I have been busy reviewing notes from my meetings  and interviews. During my twenty-plus hours in Charlotte, I met with the entire Capital Cargo Data Center senior management team and interviewed all the key members of the technical and project staff. In summary, about half of what I discovered and observed was not surprising. However, the other half was quite disturbing.

First, here is the half that was not surprising.

> The consolidation of four older regional data centers into the new Charlotte Data Center concluded about six months ago. Prior to this consolidation effort, Capital Cargo had not experienced a daylong outage of their online banking system in over 10 years.

> When I arrived at the Charlotte Data Center Friday morning, the first thing I discovered was that, since the consolidation project's completion, most of the Charlotte team has been working through numerous problems with the installation of new server technology, the upgrade of old technology and a massive data migration effort. All of this was in addition to the normal activity associated with data center operations.

> Because of the magnitude of the consolidation effort and the new skill sets required to integrate the disparate systems, the project required a significant amount of leadership presence to sort through the available skills and competences of the Data Center's technical and project staff.

> Based on my Data Center experience, I knew that the key to any successful consolidation effort of this type is to have a comprehensive integration strategy and work plans at all levels of the organization.

> Not surprising, throughout the data center facility, I found a dedicated and committed technical and project staff. They were working long hours and overtime was abundant. I have learned over the years that this situation frequently occurs at the end of most large system integration and data migration projects. Therefore, these initial findings were not a surprise.

However, it soon became apparent to me that the team's major challenges were three-fold: 1) the lack of a comprehensive problem resolution strategy; 2) the lack of an organizational-wide work plan; and 3) the lack of an adequate level of leadership presence. For me to discover major gaps in *strategic, tactical and operational leadership* — months after system "go live" — was quite unusual. The absence of attention and presence at all three of these levels of leadership in a corporation the size of Capital Cargo was unthinkable.

Now, here is the other half of what I discovered and observed at the Charlotte Data Center. This is the part that astonishingly, left me both surprised and quite disturbed.

Although the Capital Cargo Data Center senior management team included experienced technologist and managers, it was apparent during my visit that this particular team lacked the senior leadership skills required to lead such a complex and multi-facetted consolidation. The turnover rate of both the project management and technical staff had increased significantly over the last few months. After only a few hours at the Center, I could sense a general feeling of desperation at all levels of the organization.

A couple of senior team leads shared with me during private interviews that, starting a few months ago, the sense of desperation seemed to have increased sharply. This was about the same time that most members of the middle management team began to feel that they *had to* and were *expected to* spend most of their time on the operations floor to help "do the work".

During my discussions with the team's project managers, I discovered that a few members of the senior management team did stay in the position to recognize global integration issues surrounding the consolidation project. They also had the authority to quickly shift or add the skills and resources required to resolve issues more proactively. However, after multiple requests by several project managers, they failed to do so.

In conclusion, it became clear to me that there was simply not a sufficient level of senior leadership presence throughout the Charlotte Data Center organization. Without such presence, it was nearly impossible to develop a  winning level of cohesiveness, gain concurrence on an overall resolution strategy and create the organizational momentum required for the Charlotte Center to be successful — and outage free.

****

On Monday morning, I submitted what I believe was an honest and very comprehensive report to Ralph Dean and the Capital Cargo executive team, as promised.

The cover page of my report included:

Report on the Charlotte Data Center Performance Challenge

Root Cause: Senior Leadership Missing in Action

Solution: Leadership Training and/or New Leaders Needed

****

A few weeks later, while heading home from work, I received the following text message from Ralph Dean:

"Thanks, AJ. Good job. Just as I suspected. An astonishing lack of leadership presence. It was an extremely difficult Board meeting last month. New leadership team now in place at the Charlotte Data Center. Corporate-wide leadership training sessions will start soon."

Questions to Ponder

1. How would you describe Ralph Dean's situation?

2. How would you describe AJ's situation?

3. Why do you believe Ralph Dean confided in AJ and asked for his perspective on the issues with the Charlotte Data Center?

4. Ralph's instincts told him that his executive team's explanation of the problem "*simply don't hold water.*"

    How much should you depend on your instincts in determining how you should address a specific situation?

5. How much did AJ's background help him "cut through the chase" and quickly get to the "root cause" in this situation?

6. Even though the senior management team in Charlotte was in the Data Center, why do you think AJ defined the root cause of the problem as "Senior Leadership Missing in Action" ?

7. While AJ described the Data Center technical and project staff as "dedicated and committed", as a team, the Data Center Staff still did not do enough to properly address the situation.

    Why should you look beyond people "being right but not doing the right things" to effectively manage challenging situations?

What are some of the lessons you should take away from this story and situation?

1. I must be present with my presence (knowledge, insights, experience, empathy and leadership skills) to ensure that the outcomes of challenging situations are positive and meets expectations.
2.
3.
4.
5.
6.
7.
8.

CHAPTER SIX

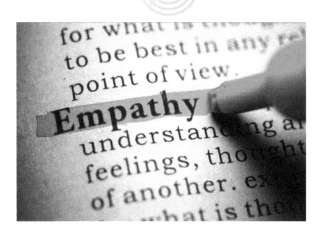

I DIDN'T EXPECT THIS

My name is Rebecca Bushman. In January of this year, I was promoted to a Regional Vice President of Sales for Roland Pharmaceuticals. Roland Pharmaceuticals currently distributes over a thousand various pharmaceutical products to doctor offices and hospitals in the Rocky Mountain region of the United States.

Today is December 14th and there are ten business days remaining in this year. During this time of the year when most people are getting into the holiday spirit, I found myself shedding *tears of misery* and feeling a touch of depression while driving into my office this morning.

However, starting early this afternoon, I experienced a series of unexpected and welcomed events. Because of these timely events, I am now crying giant *tears of joy*.

53

Wow. This has been quite a journey. Through it all, I still can't believe that I was deprived of the opportunity, during my years of leadership training, to learn such a powerful *skill* and *competency*.

What were the circumstances that helped to navigate my journey and brought me to this nexus of *relief* and *disbelief* — and what is this powerful *skill* and *competency?*

****

Well. This journey began around five years ago when I started working for Roland Pharmaceuticals. I first met and became friends with the company's owners, Bob and Jennifer Roland over ten years ago.

We were all working on our MBA degrees at Denver College at the time. They both were ambitious and entrepreneurial. They talked constantly about one day owning a product distribution company.

As fate would have it, around seven years ago, Bob and Jenifer were able to purchase the assets of a bankrupt Denver-based Pharmaceutical distributor. I was so excited when I heard that Bob and Jennifer had bought the assets and had successfully launched the new entity as Roland Pharmaceuticals. Within two years of operation, they were successful in adequately capitalizing the new startup by gaining the financial support of a venture capital investment group with the exchange of 48% ownership in the company.

Not long after the investors were in place, I met Bob and Jennifer for dinner. They were still thrilled and excited. I congratulated them and inquired how things were going. During our conversation, I mentioned that I would be interested in joining the company at some point. A couple of weeks later, Jennifer called and offered me a position. I accepted the offer, left my sales management position with a major wholesale distribution company, and joined Roland Pharmaceuticals as a Senior Sales Representative.

Last year, Roland's year-over-year sales revenue increased by 43% and exceeded the $100 million mark for the first time while operating in only half of the country. It was not a secret that Roland's investment partners were interested in taking the company public via an Initial Public Offering (IPO). The goal was to raise the cash needed to expand operations nation-wide and capture some of the return on their investment.

In January of this year, as a part of the preparation for an IPO, the company appointed four new Regional Vice Presidents, including myself. We were all given a hefty number of Class B shares of Roland stock and were tasked with leading our perspective sales regions, and Roland Pharmaceuticals, to one more year of significant product sales growth. Our success would set the stage for pulling the trigger on the Roland IPO and the opportunity for the company to reward the leadership team for the long hours and hard work.

****

Now, the reason I am sitting here tonight at my desk crying big *tears of joy* instead of *tears of misery* is due to a set of attention-grabbing circumstances. Together, these circumstances would, contribute to both my success and my professional growth.

The circumstances surfaced in July of this year. This was during the part of my journey that brought me unforeseen worry and concern.

Unbelievably, almost simultaneously, all three of my top Sales Representatives, Sheniqua, Santiago and Meaghan were beset with extraordinary health, family and personal challenges.

In June of this year, my sales region was over 100% of plan. The morale and spirit of my entire sales team were through the roof. Everyone felt confident that we would meet or exceed our sales quota this year. By doing so, my region would do its part to help Roland Pharmaceuticals have another great sales year.

Since Denver was my largest metropolitan area, all three of my top Sales Representatives were in my greater Denver sales territory. It was not a surprise that the trio was responsible for over 80% of my region's product sales during the first half of the year. Each had contributed about a quarter of my region's sales through June.

It was just after the long July 4th weekend, when Sheniqua was the first of the three to approach me. She entered my office Tuesday morning profusely apologizing for having missed several sales calls at two major hospitals last week due to family problems. She later learned that her customer contacts were not incredibly happy with her right now. She inferred that she might miss her third quarter sales quota. To be totally honest, the first thing I thought was *"Well, this is what I have been afraid of since I hired her"*.

Sheniqua shared that she and her three young children had been sleeping in her van for the past few nights. She and her husband have been dealing with some irreconcilable differences in their marriage for over a year and she had finally decided to leave him and get a divorce. However, for now, she needed a few weeks off to get herself together; to find a place for her and the kids to stay; and to get back to being her old self. Having never experienced or been around any situation like this, I said, *"I am so sorry to hear this, Sheniqua. Let me think about this situation and I will get back with you tomorrow.*"

Later that afternoon, Santiago's wife, Isabella, called me and shared the news that he had to be taken to the emergency room when he suddenly collapsed at home after dinner. Fortunately, it was only a mild stroke and his doctor said that he should recover fully. However, he would most likely have to miss work for at least a

month. Again, my self-talk kicked in and I said to myself, *"I have always felt that he was too overweight and seemed to get too stressed out over minor things. I would have bet that he would end up in this condition."*

Having almost recovered from my conversation earlier with Sheniqua, I just took a deep breath and said, *"Isabella, I am so sorry to hear this. Glad to hear that Santiago will fully recover. Give him my best. Please let him know that I will get with him later this week, when he is better, and discuss how to manage his sales territory."*

 As I was driving home that evening, wondering what else can go wrong today, my cell phone rang, and I noticed it was **Meaghan** calling. After I arrived home and relaxed, I listened to Meaghan's voice message.

She wanted to share that her eighty-three-year-old mother's health had taken a turn for the worst. Her mother was suffering from an advanced case of dementia and had been admitted to a memory care facility a few months ago.

Somehow, her mother was able to walk away alone from the facility this morning. Fortunately, they were able to find her a few miles down the street. **Meaghan** said that her mother was now safe and okay. However, since she was the only child, she had to fly down to Miami tomorrow morning to determine what she needed to do about the situation. Then she added, *"I am not sure how long I must be away from work."* I thought, *"I can really relate with Meaghan's disturbing situation. I lost my mother to the dreadful condition a few years ago and Meaghan has been such an excellent sales performer."*

After I thought about Meaghan's unfortunate circumstance for a few minutes, I returned the call to let her know that I had received her message. I told her that I was so sorry to hear the news about her mother and asked if there was anything, I could do to help. Following a lengthy conversation, I agreed to personally take over her sales calls until she was able to return to work.

Then, I suddenly began to panic a little when I realized how unthinkable it would be for me to disappoint Bob and Jennifer. I knew that, as my organization's leader, I had to make some good decisions regarding the feedback I must give Sheniqua and Santiago. More importantly, I also must craft a plan to make sure that my sales region achieves its annual sales quota.

Feeling a bit professionally overwhelmed, I made an appointment with my long-time career coach, Fred Miller. I met with Fred early the next morning over a cup of coffee.

After dumping on Fred, the details of my current dilemma and my conversations with Sheniqua, Santiago and Meaghan, he began to patiently coach me through this untravelled leadership challenge as follows:

- Fred took the time to walk me through not only *what he thought I was saying* but also *how he thought I was feeling*.
  I must admit that although I have worked with Fred for years, this was the first that I noticed how deeply he listened and how well he understood me.

- He shared with me that based on what he had heard — he was not concerned with me being able to handle the "management" challenges that accompanied this type of dilemma. However, he was genuinely concerned whether

I would be able to generate and wrap the proper amount of *"empathy"* around all my new leadership challenges.

- Fred explained that along with the triad of challenges associated with Sheniqua, Santiago and Meaghan, a fourth new leadership challenge has also surfaced. The fourth challenge involves how I would maintain the morale and spirit of the rest of my organization — considering the possibly crippling effect of missing the top three sales reps for an extended period.

- Fred mentioned that while he was listening to the rundown of my conversation with Meaghan, he clearly sensed that I was able to be sincerely *empathetic* with her situation.

   He added, *"What I mean is that it appears that you were able to put yourself in Meaghan's shoes and completely understand her situation. Thus, you quickly made the decision on how you would treat her and her circumstance."*

- He shared that he also gathered from my conversations with Sheniqua and Santiago that, unlike Meaghan's circumstance, their similar level of concerns appeared to be totally foreign to me.

   Fred surprised me when he said, *"Not only did I sense a degree of unfamiliarity, but I also picked up on a little more than a touch of stereotyping. This is a combination which serves to make it very difficult for anyone to be empathetic and to reap the dividends to be gained from being an empathetic leader."*

- Fred managed to get and keep my undivided attention as he described the important role that a *leader's empathy* plays in developing and effectively managing workplace relationships. He walked me through how leaders lacking empathy are driven by their own needs. They also become blind or indifferent to the needs of others.

- In addition, Fred wanted to make sure that I was aware that all my other team members would be closely watching how I handled the unfortunate circumstances that have beset Sheniqua, Santiago and Meaghan. If they sense a genuine display of empathy from me, in handling all three circumstances, it will serve to energize and gain their support.

I left this unusually long, yet quite enlightening, coaching session with a plan. The primary leadership trait I would have to rely on was, without a doubt, one that was not familiar to me. However, I felt I had to trust the advice Fred had given me.

For the next five months, I studied what I should be doing as an empathic leader. I literally had to force myself to make the personal and professional changes necessary. I felt that I had no choice. I had to generate the level of empathy required to help me better understand and react to all four of my new leadership challenges — the unforeseen challenges that had just rocked my world.

I spent more time with Sheniqua and Santiago to get to know them better and to learn more about what it would be like to walk in their shoes. I suddenly realized how little I knew about their lives outside of the workplace. I was very unaware of the personal strengths that keeps them going daily — strengths that I had simply overlooked.

I budgeted time in my schedule to personally keep the entire team informed of how the organization was supporting Sheniqua, Santiago and Meaghan and how they were recovering from their extraordinary personal, health and family challenges.

I used weekly team-wide communications meetings and the posting of weekly performance metrics to keep everyone involved in the year-end sales push.

Consequently, I became closer to all my team members and, I found myself experiencing some of the best times I have ever had as a Sales Manager.

****

So, you see, during my drive into the office this morning, all I could think about was the $10 million dollars of revenue that my sales region needed to bring in during the ten business days remaining in the month and the fiscal year. The *tears of misery* began to flow about halfway through my drive in. That is when I finally realized how difficult it was going to be to bring in another $10 million dollars of sales this late in the year.

I was not surprised that we had gotten this close despite our poor third quarter sales performance. Once Sheniqua, Santiago and Meaghan were able to *spring back* into action and the rest of the sales team was able to exceed their prior year sales numbers during September and October, I felt we at least had a small chance to get close to reaching our goal. Historically, after the middle of December, the only year-end sales opportunities available were from customers who needed to purchase critical supplies, and these were generally small orders.

However, to my astonishment, around noon today a series of unexpected events began to transpire. Meaghan called a little before 1:00 PM and shared that she was able to convince two of her largest hospitals to stock up early for the coming year. This meant that she would be able to pull a new $3 million order into this fiscal year.

Around 3:00 PM Santiago called and left me a message, which stated: *"Great news Rebecca. I was able to meet with ten of my largest doctor offices last week. Together, I expect get at least $4 million of new orders. All of the orders should become additional sales and be recorded before the end of the year".*

I was so excited at this point. I literally jumped up and ran over to my manager's building to share the good news. I informed him that our chances of reaching our annual sales quota had increased significantly through the efforts of Meaghan and Santiago.

Almost breathless, I returned to my office building around 4:00 PM. To my surprise, I was told that Sheniqua was in my office waiting for me. As I walked in, she jumped to her feet with one finger in the air and said, *"Guess what Ms. B. Here it is. I got it."* Sheniqua handed me a confirmed order for $3.5 million of unplanned sales. She had spent all week, working late into the evenings to make sure that the sales are recorded this year.

As I finally caught my breathe, I began to realize that Sheniqua's additional $3.5 million of sales, combined with the $7 million of new sales reported by Meaghan and Santiago, would give us more than the $10 million dollars needed to meet our annual sales goal.

I ran over to Sheniqua and gave her a big hug, for the very first time.

****

Again, here I am. I am still sitting here in my office at the nexus of *relief* and *disbelief*. However, I am no longer mystified by why *empathy*, in the hands of an organizational leader, is such a powerful *skill* and *competency*.

I am so proud of everyone for making the extraordinary effort required to *spring back* and do what was necessary to get a win here, including yours truly.

However, I must admit…*I didn't expect this.*

Questions to Ponder

1. How would you describe Rebecca's situation?

2. Why was Rebecca able to quickly understand Meagan's situation and struggled with comprehending Santiago and Sheniqua's situations.

3. What role did the need for more "self-awareness" play in effectively addressing Rebecca's situation?

4. Why do you think it is important in all situations for you to be able to listen and respond to others with empathy?

5. How can being professionally empathetic increase teamwork and decrease conflicts in most situations?

6. What suggestions made in Rebecca's coaching session with Fred can you apply to anyone faced with challenging situations and why?

7. What dividends or bonuses can you expect when you apply empathetic skills to challenging situations?

What are some of the lessons you should take away from this story and situation?

1. By being professionally empathetic of others who are involved in resolving a challenging situation, I will not only make better decisions but will also gain the dividends associated with increased wisdom and a broader perspective.
2.
3.
4.
5.
6.
7.
8.

CHAPTER SEVEN

NOW, IT MAKES SENSE

I was born at 11: 43 PM on Christmas Eve in 1967.

When I was born, my mother was six feet tall, in her late thirties and on her way to becoming a distinguished professor at a highly respected private university. My father was six feet five. He retired as the first Hispanic American Sergeant Major of the Army the same year I was born. He has since climbed the ladder to become a Commander in our state's largest police department.

65

As early as when I entered kindergarten, I came to grips with three of my life's realities. As it turned out, these three realities have subconsciously guided my progression through my 27-year career. They, without doubt, have also contributed greatly to the reason why I am sitting on this stage today.

The first reality is that, due to my parent's age when I was born, I soon realized that I would grow up as an only child.

The second reality is that I would always be a "girly girl" and would always enjoy competing against the boys.

The third became obvious when I inherited by grandmother's height of only about five feet four and became aware of my parent's significant professional accomplishments. Thus, I realized that I would always, literally and figuratively, be looking up to my parents.

Now, growing up in a family as the only child took its toll. One of the most challenging ordeals for me as a kid was the fact that it was nearly impossible for me to get away with anything.

However, having my parent's constant and undivided attention meant that I was able to avoid getting into any real trouble. I spent most of my time focusing on school instead of parties. Being an only child allowed me to be able to develop unique relationships with both of my parents. Most likely it would have been different if had I shared them with siblings.

Growing up as a "girly girl" allowed me to maintain interesting interpersonal and romantic relationships with the boys. But then again, I have never been afraid to tell my male classmates and coworkers that they are being sexist. My mother noticed this trait in me early in my life. She would often say *"Celestina, be strong, but be fair."*

I must confess it is my relationship with both of my parents and a single piece of advice that my father gave me six years ago that is the primary reason I am sitting here today.

Just before I left Phoenix, with some hesitation, for my first and only out-of-state job opportunity, my father shared with me the following:

"Remember Celestina, if you want to become the best at what you do and stand on the biggest stages; don't focus on whether or not you will be successful. Instead, for every door that opens, you should go through it focusing on mastering every aspect of the job and becoming a masterful leader — your ultimate success will depend upon what happens when you leave the room."

To be honest, I am quite nervous right now. You see, in few minutes, my name, Celestina Deloris Rodriguez, will be called. I will then stand, walk over to the mayor, raise my right hand, and take the oath to become the first female chief of the largest police department in the state.

This means that a little girl named Celestina has grown up and has earned the opportunity to be called "Chief Rodriguez". This will be a first in my family. As the Chief of the Phoenix Police Department, I will lead an organization with over 2,500 sworn officers and more than 800 civilian employees along with an annual budget that exceeds $450 million.

How did I get here?

Let me first share with you a brief chronological breakdown of the "stops" along the way and "leadership growth" required of me to pull it all off. Then, I will share why my father's wise advice was so valuable and why it now makes sense.

****

67

In 1989, I graduated with from Arizona State University with a Bachelor of Arts degree in Public Administration and joined the Phoenix Police Department as a Patrol Officer.

Not surprising, I followed my father into a law enforcement career. When I was a freshman in high school, I told my father that my goal was to become at least a Department Commander like him. Secretly, I established a career goal of becoming the first Phoenix Police Department's female Police Chief.

My initial goal, as a Patrol Officer, was to earn the recognition of the current Police Department leadership team as being an outstanding performer. I knew that to reach the top of the leadership ranks, I would have to learn all aspects of the law enforcement profession and develop the leadership skills required to master what it takes to lead a large department.

I made a commitment to myself that would require me to treat my leadership development as seriously as all the other aspects of my professional life. I decided that at each new level of responsibility, I would *develop* and *execute* a leadership growth plan.

The plan would outline what I had to learn and how I would strategically deploy my new management and leadership skills. I also wanted to make sure that my plan included the specific actions required to develop the leadership culture I wanted to leave behind when I moved on.

In 1994, I completed graduate school with a master's degree in Education with an emphasis on leadership development and crisis management. I received the promotion to Lieutenant in October of the same year.

68

As a Lieutenant, I now had the responsibility for helping officers with situations that required seniority or expertise in the field. My leadership growth plan at this "stop" required me to do two things:

1. Build trust with each team member by having the courage to speak the truth on all matters; and

2. Demonstrate flexibility in my behavior.

I decided to become more flexible in my thinking and decision making by working on enhancing my personal level of emotional intelligence. I could instantly see improvement in my ability to perceive, understand and manage my emotions more accurately. I also took advantage of this newfound ability to understand the emotions of my team members. During my role as a Lieutenant, I received several internal recognitions for the level of trust that existed throughout my organizations.

In 1999, I became a Commander within the Phoenix Police Department. As a Commander, I was now responsible for overseeing day-to-day operations and personnel. This included preparing budgets; recommending personnel and capital needs; and directing or personally investigating citizen complaints about Police personnel conduct and service.

As a Commander, I was now responsible for leading a much larger organization. My leadership growth plan at this "stop" required me to do three things:

1. Maintain my organization's trust by being accountable for my team's results while helping to identify and implement solutions for improvement. I would depend on this action to encourage loyalty and excellence.

2. Work on increasing my leadership presence and influence throughout the Department. This action would help me to positively influence my team to embrace organizational goals without feeling any pressure or fear; and

3. Budget the time into my busy schedule so that I could spend some quality moments with my teams and exhibit the appropriate level of professional empathy in all situations — especially those that recognize the risk that my officers must take every day to do their jobs.

After a few months as a Commander, I noticed how my focus on being an empathetic leader was becoming contagious. I witnessed on a few occasions where my direct reports approached internal misconduct investigations in a more empathetic fashion. The culture within my organization seemed to transform into one that valued empathy coupled with responsibility.

In 2005, I received the promotion to Assistant Chief. As an Assistant Police Chief, I was responsible for assisting in the planning, directing, and coordinating all activities in the Police Department.

I worked hard to get this promotion. I knew that the new role would require longer hours and would test my ability to both effectively manage and lead at the most senior levels.

The visibility I would gain throughout city government and the Phoenix community was important for me to have a chance at becoming a future Chief of Police candidate.

My leadership growth plan at this "stop" required me to do two things:

1. Exhibit a higher level of passion. This would be at a level that would send the message to everyone saying, *"I love my work. What I do inspires me and ignites your passion"*; and

2. Take every opportunity to share the Department's mission and vision statements. This includes sharing my personal interpretation of how the vision targets quality of life improvements in all the communities in Phoenix. I felt that this was a critical action to take. I felt it was important to be viewed as a visionary leader.

In 2011, I took a big and somewhat risky step in my career. I made the difficult decision to resign from the Phoenix Police Department and accept the position of the Police Chief for the City of Oxnard, California.

This was a difficult career decision for me. During the five years since becoming a Phoenix Assistant Police Chief, I had received many internal awards and public accolades. However, I had not received any indication that I was one of the top candidates to become the next Chief.

In July 2010, a friend brought to my attention the nationwide search to find a new City of Oxnard Police Chief. After a closer look, I submitted my resume of qualification and placed myself in contention. I felt that it would at least test the strength of my resume and give me some experience in the interview process — assuming I get that far in their search.

Four months later, I had dinner with my mother and father to share with them the employment agreement I had just received to become the Police Chief for the City of Oxnard. The city of Oxnard's population was only a quarter of that of Phoenix and accordingly, the Oxnard Police Department was much smaller. There was a total of 249 sworn officers and only 129 civilians on staff.

Both my mother and father encouraged me to give the Oxnard agreement offer serious consideration. As we were leaving dinner, my mother put her arms around me and said, *"Even though the city is smaller, you will still have the responsibility of being a Chief of Police. I know how much you have put into your many years with the Phoenix PD and how you will miss the strong organizations, you have helped to build. But it is a real opportunity to get some valuable experience, my dear."*

With some hesitation and genuine disappointment for having to leave the Phoenix Police Department to achieve this next level of professional accomplishment, I accepted the offer and became the Police Chief for the City of Oxnard in February 2011.

I left Phoenix wondering if I would ever again get this close to becoming a Police Chief in one of the largest cities in the U.S.

Early in 2016, I learned that the City of Phoenix had recently initiated a nationwide search to find a new Police Chief.

This was really a surprise. I thought about the opportunity for a long time before I threw my hat in the ring. I had completed all the major objectives and goals I set when I joined the Oxnard Police Department as its Chief. Therefore, I was sure I would receive a good recommendation from the city of Oxnard. However, I was not sure how my performance during my many years in the Phoenix Police Department would come into play.

It is always easier to leave an organization than to return. The idea of returning as the organization's top leader, presents even more uncertainty. Nevertheless, what did I have to lose.

After, a short conversation with my parents, I made the phone call to request to be included in the search.

In October 2016, I was selected out of hundreds of applicants and a dozen candidates who were interviewed, to become the Police Chief for the City of Phoenix, the seventh largest city in the United States.

****

Now you know the "stops" and the events that are responsible for paving the way for me to be in the position to take this oath today.

So, let me get back to the advice that my father gave me six years ago and the primary reason I am sitting on this stage.

As you recall my father told me that, *"I should go through the doors of all opportunities focusing on mastering every aspect of the job and becoming a masterful leader — my ultimate success will depend upon what happens when I leave the room."*

After I was selected as the successful candidate, the chairperson of the City of Phoenix Search Committee shared with me the following.

"The strong recommendations we received from all of the teams that you led and organizations that you were a part of during your prior twenty-two years with the city of Phoenix Police Department clearly separated you from all of the other candidates. We heard many superlatives describing you and your outstanding performance as a leader. Probably the two that impressed us the most were that you were a masterful leader and that you were remarkably successful in all the positions you held."

While reflecting on this feedback, I began to realize what my father meant when he told me, *"success happens when you leave the room"*.

Now, it makes sense.

Questions to Ponder

1. How would you describe Celestina's approach to both managing her career "stops" and addressing the situations she encountered along the way?

2. Celestina developed a plan for each "stop" in her career.

   How can creating a plan help you more effectively address many of the situations you may encounter?

3. What role did Celestina's vision for her future play in being prepared to deal with the situations she would face?

4. What are the most common situations that can benefit from understanding that "success happens when you leave the room"?

5. Celestina's relationship with her family was an integral part of her success.

   How can maintaining healthy relationships within the workplace also help you manage challenging situations more effectively?

6. Have you had any experiences where you have benefited from the positive impressions you made in prior roles or situations?

74

What are some of the lessons you should take away from this story and situation?

1. Because in many cases my success could be dependent on what happens "when I leave the room", I will make sure that I clearly make my desires and expectations known prior to leaving any discussions or meetings involved in positively resolving challenging situations.
2.
3.
4.
5.
6.
7.
8.

"Your current situation is no indication of your ultimate potential"

~ Tony Robbins

Anthony Jay Robbins is an American author, coach, motivational speaker, and philanthropist. Robbins is known for his infomercials, seminars, and self-help books including the books Unlimited Power and Awaken the Giant Within.

CHAPTER EIGHT

THE TREES GOT ME

My name is Larry Dean.

Twenty-four hours ago, I was the Lead Supervisor of the Flight Information System and Training Department for Miracle Mile Aerospace. I am now sitting at my desk in my home office, working on an updated resume while goggling "goals", "strategy" and "tactics". As I have recently and painfully learned, it's never too late to make sure you have a firm grasp of the fundamentals.

If this doesn't make sense to you, you're not alone.

77

Here's a little background on a dreadful situation. In hindsight, it is a situation I could have avoided by simply realizing that, even within organizations, winning the battles doesn't always win the war.

Over the past five months, I have spent six days a week and ten hours a day leading a major company initiative. At the outset, I was convinced that this effort would lead to accolades for my team and a promotion for me. Instead, I was removed from my Department Supervisor's position two weeks ago. Then I was dismissed from the company yesterday morning. The reasons given were *"your inability to perform at the required level and your failure to maintain internal safety practices."*

I still believe that my firing was due more to the political pressure that Miracle Mile was receiving because of the two recent airplane mishaps, but I will never really know. Fortunately, no lives were lost. What I do know is that up until it all "hit the fan" two weeks ago, I sincerely believed I was winning the battles and doing exactly what was expected of me.

78

During my exit interview yesterday, Gloria Hawkins, the Director of Human Resources, agreed that the company's strategy for implementing the initiative may not have been clearly articulated during the later stages of its rollout. In her words, *"Jimmy John, the Chief Operating Officer, could have done a better job communicating the fundamental challenges associated with the initiative's financial success and the need to maintain operational safety."* Then she added, *"However Larry, it has to be assumed that someone at your level of responsibility should have been able to understand these fundamentals and certainly not risk the possibility of a major safety mishap.*

Now, here is what I did, what I didn't do and what I learned.

****

What I did.

This new initiative was code-named, "Safety And More Profits" or SAMP for short. I was aware that versions of the SAMP initiative had been launched successfully in three other departments prior to being launched in my Flight Information System and Training (FISAT) Department in June of this year. Everyone talked about how the Supervisors of those three departments quickly received grade promotions because of their success.

In a meeting with the COO during the initiative kick-off, I learned that FISAT would be the last department to launch SAMP this fiscal year. All three of the prior departments were responsible for a variety of flight control hardware upgrades. As a part of the SAMP initiative, certain "safety upgrades" were to now be sold as "optional" safety features on new airplanes and "upgrade options" to existing airlines currently flying Miracle Mile aircraft.

I heard through the grapevine that all three of the prior departments had met or exceeded the anticipated financial targets for "safety option" sales. The metric used to determine their "success" was documented in a new company report titled, *New Safety Options Sales Strategy and Guidelines.*

Unfortunately, I didn't receive a copy of the new report. I did make a note to myself to review a copy. But, of course, I never got around to reviewing a copy and gaining more insight into the initiative's rollout strategy. Based on my twenty years of experience, I felt comfortable with my vision of how to proceed and be successful with the SAMP initiative launch in my department.

After attending several additional meetings with the COO, I surmised that if the SAMP rollout was also successful in my department, it would help Miracle Mile meet its overall financial goal for the fiscal year. I also assumed it would help me get the expected grade promotion.

So, based on what I knew at this point about the initiative, I established the goals, implementation strategy and operational tactics we would use to successfully launch SAMP within my organization.

The primary goal was to identify as many opportunities to rollback once "standard" safety documentation features as possible. These features would then be sold as "safety options" going forward.

My strategy was to have our sales team use recent "feature use data history" to support why the features are now considered optional to existing customers. Then, we would offer the safety features as options on all new Miracle Mile aircraft. In addition, I decided to offer a special discount on "safety option" sales to existing airlines currently operating without the safety features.

I spent hours devising the operational tactics to ensure that we met the anticipated sales goal for our "safety options" this fiscal year.

In an all-hands meeting, I instructed my team to increase the number of safety feature option sales by first, systematically contacting all the airlines operating Miracle Mile planes and discussing airplane safety. Then, using a written script that I had developed, they were to make a *hard sales push* and persuade the airline to purchase the optional safety documentation for their existing flight information systems.

The internal battles started when a few of my team leads began to express concerns regarding the lack of certain pilot navigation documentation on Miracle Mile planes flying into airports with short runways. They suggested several different approaches to rolling out the SAMP initiative in our department. Some of their suggestions even involved taking pilot surveys and waiting for pilot feedback.

Because most of what the team suggested would extend the SAMP initiative rollout beyond the end of the fiscal year, I overruled the suggestions and eventually won all these battles by forcefully instructing everyone to move full speed ahead.

Up until two weeks ago, it appeared that we were being successful by exceeding the number of anticipated customer contacts and "safety option" sales. Then, it all "hit the fan".

Two airlines flying new Miracle Mile planes out of small airports were forced to make emergency landings. One incident involved a near mid-air collision with another plane preparing to land. The forced landings were caused by a navigation alert that was traced back to a latent hardware defect in a pilot control assist device. The device could have been easily overridden in flight, if the pilots of those planes had the safety documentation required in their flight information system. The documentation in question was, of course, a part of the safety documentation that my department had offered to both airlines only as a "safety option".

****

What I didn't do.

As I sit here today and reflect on the past five months, I can now see clearly what went wrong.

Without any doubt, I worked hard on planning and leading every aspect of the SAMP initiative rollout in my department. I spent a lot of time thinking through the details and making what I thought were good assumptions about what was being asked of me and what was required for me and my team to be successful.

However, in hindsight, it was not what I did, but what I didn't do that caused this dreadful situation. Here is what I didn't do and what would have made a difference in the outcome.

1. I didn't realize that my role as Lead Supervisor required me to make sure that I clearly understood my company's

top-level strategies and to determine how to incorporate them into what my organization was being asked to do.

My failure to read the company's report on the SAMP initiative, denied me the opportunity to "see the big picture". If I had read the report, I would have been aware that it strongly emphasized the following, *"A key component of a successful SAMP initiative implementation strategy is for all department leaders to be extremely mindful of NOT sacrificing aircraft operational safety. Remember, operational safety trumps option sales."*

2. I didn't listen to my team leads when they expressed concerns about the potential flight safety of some aircraft. Instead, I remained in the "bowels" of the initiative's implementation. By doing so, I considered my experts' feedback, as "competition" to my plans. Unfortunately, I lost sight of the "war" and made sure that I would win all of the "battles".

3. In my meeting with my senior management, I didn't have the wherewithal and the courage to directly ask some important questions about the company's SAMP initiative rollout strategy and flight safety concerns within my department.

   I should have made sure that the COO was aware of the unique challenges associated with selecting and selling "safety options" in flight information systems versus other types of system upgrades. I should have known that, as the most knowledgeable person in the room on this topic, I was expected to provide leadership in this area.

4. I failed to gather the level of emotional intelligence needed at the time to effectively lead my team. I should not have allowed the possibility of "accolades for my team and a promotion for me" to overshadow the clarity of my thinking, planning and motivation. In hindsight, I now see

that all my plans, goals, strategy and tactics targeted "option sales" and not flight safety.

As Gloria Hawkins, the Director of Human Resources, pointed out, *"someone at my level of responsibility should have been able to understand these fundamentals."*

****

What I learned.

I must admit that I am embarrassed about what I learned or should I say, "once again learned".

Even though I am aware of the need to think and plan based on sound "goals", "strategy" and "tactics", I was reminded that leaders must also approach the development of goals, strategy and tactics with a focus on the "forest" and not the "trees".

Simply put, in this case, *the trees got me.*

Questions to Ponder

1. How would you describe Larry's situation?

2. Reflecting on past situations you have been faced with, list some things you "didn't do" that may have exasperated conflicts with others?

3. What leadership fundamentals did Larry Dean ignore?

4. Why do you think Larry missed the importance of focusing on the organization's broadest objectives (i.e., the "forest) and not just the operational details (i.e., the trees)?

5. When chosen to be the leader, why is it your primary responsibility to make sure that the battles fought contribute to winning the ultimate goals and objectives?

6. Why is it important to have the wherewithal and the courage to directly ask important questions and gain the proper perspective when involved in making decisions in challenging situations?

What are some of the lessons you should take away from this story and situation?

1. Knowing that winning the battles doesn't always win the war, I will always make sure that I focus on the broadest objectives of the situation at hand and not be misdirected by irrelevant details.
2.
3.
4.
5.
6.
7.
8.

CHAPTER NINE

I Only Needed To Be Like Mike

It was a *very close call.*

However, Charlie Yang is still the President and CEO of the Better Way Foundation. As the CEO, he oversees the National Office and all Branch Operations.

I am a long-time member of the Better Way Foundation Board of Directors. I was the Chairman of the Board eight year ago when Charlie was selected after a national search to become only the second President of the twenty-five-year-old organization.

The Founding President and CEO, Michael (Mike) Monahan, lost his fight with cancer a little more than a year earlier. Mike founded the Better Way Foundation when he was only 24 years old. Over the years, Mike became a trusted leader and was greatly admired by the entire organization.

Let me first share a little history of the organization.

Then, I will explain why it was such a close call for Charlie to retain his job, secure a new five-year employment agreement and, more importantly, regain the trust of the organization that once viewed him as the "second coming of Mike".

The first branch of the Better Way Foundation was founded in 1974 as a community-based, non-profit organization. The multi-million-dollar organization currently has seventy-four local Branch Offices located throughout the United States.

The Better Way promotes and supports the common good in small communities with a focus on education, income and health—the building blocks for a better way of life.

Each Better Way Branch Office has a Director, a small staff and a local Advisory Board selected from highly respected members of the community. The National Office of the foundation manages the operational performance and governance of all Branch Offices. Each Branch works closely with the National Office and administers all local programs and initiatives.

This quasi-decentralized management and leadership approach has achieved national acclaim. The approach is considered the primary reason the non-profit has been able to expand so rapidly and garner so much success in accomplishing its mission.

With the rapid growth of new Branch Offices, the founding President made it a priority in his work schedule to visit each Branch at least every other month. Mike often shared, with anyone who would listen, his leadership motto. The motto was even on the back of his business card and read, *"Listen First, Talk Straight, Right Wrongs and Extend Trust."*

Everyone was aware of Mike's leadership style and preparation. Prior to each Branch visit, he would make sure that he was knowledgeable of the Branch's ongoing activities and unique challenges. His visits always included time for him to personally establish, grow, extend and, if needed, restore trust with Branch Directors and their staff.

During his meetings, Mike would stress the need for each Branch Director to inspire and maintain a high level of trust and credibility. These face-to-face coaching sessions revealed Mike's passion and motivated the Branch Directors to eagerly follow his lead. At times, he would privately share with me that the, near weekly, trips were physically exhausting but as he would put it, *"inspiring and maintaining mutual trust should be job one for anyone who leads any type of organization."*

Immediately after assuming the role of the Better Way's President, Charlie visited each of the Branch Offices and met with the Directors. He made sure, that before he ended the visit, he would ask each Director the same question, *"What do you expect of me as the new Better Way President and CEO?"*

In all cases, his notes would reflect the same answer, *"you should be like Mike."*

During the first four years as President, Charlie met all the Board's expectations. He followed the advice of his Branch Directors. He was very much *"like Mike"* and the performance of the organization didn't miss a beat. As the result of his winning performance, the board offered Charlie a second four-year employment agreement.

****

Now, as I understand it, about six months after signing the new employment agreement, Charlie hired the services of a well-

89

known executive coaching firm. He was apparently growing tired of the extensive travel. He was also concerned about the increasing cost of operations. Charlie felt he needed some advice on how he could modify the current organizational leadership approach. The goal was to make the entire organization less dependent on his presence and more cost efficient.

After spending about three months working with his coach to develop a plan, Charlie announced the National Office's new leadership strategy and organizational changes.

The announcement was communicated to all seventy-four Branch Directors in the form of a series of three mass emails.

The first email detailed the reasoning for the need to modify the Better Way's leadership approach. In the same email, he revealed his new leadership motto, *"Decentralize, Reduce Operational Cost and Grow Foundation Reserves."*

The second email announced the change of his personal Branch visits from bi-monthly to once a year. It also announced the establishment of a new monthly Branch Conference Call. The call would include all Better Way Branch Directors and would be limited to one hour. The National Office would develop the agenda based on what it perceived as the month's top priorities.

The third email announced a proposal he was preparing to submit to the Better Way Foundation Board of Directors within a few months. He was proposing the closure of at least twenty-five Branch Offices over the next three years.

****

The announcement and the abrupt changes were a real shock to the entire organization. The other members the Better Way Board of Directors first learned of Charlie's organizational changes when I forwarded them the emails that one of the Branch Directors shared with me following a long and surprising phone conversation.

****

What occurred over the next three and a half years within the Better Way organization can best be described as *"a chaotic and predicable performance melt down"*.

Here is a brief summation of the major occurrences.

- The Better Way Board of Directors was disappointed that they didn't receive a briefing on the plan and the announcement prior to its release. They also felt that Charlie should have chosen a more personal method to announce such a major organizational change.

- However, to support Charlie and give his new plan a chance, the Better Way Board agreed with the idea of closing some Branch offices. As anticipated, this part of the announcement created a high degree of discomfort among the Branch Directors and their staff.

- During the first few months of the Branch Conference Call, the Branch Directors asked dozens of questions in the hope of clarifying the confusion surrounding the new decentralized Branch Office operating approach. Charlie indicated that he would get back with them. However, and unfortunately, he rarely did.

- It didn't take long for the monthly conference call to turn into a monologue. Charlie would share his concerns regarding Branch performance issues and the Branch Directors soon learned to simply, just listen.

- The lack of clear direction from the National Office and unreliable responses to their questions forced the Branch Directors to go it alone and to implement inconsistent local operating procedures.

- Charlie soon noticed that during his annual Branch Office visits, the meetings with the Directors and staff began to get shorter and more formal. Once casual, open and candid discussions were now rehearsed PowerPoint presentations.

- The monthly Branch Conference Call quickly morphed into heated discussions about methods to reduce Branch Office overhead cost, to better utilize local office staff and to improve Branch cost performance.

- Two years after launching the changes, no Branch Offices were closed, and the Foundation's overhead cost had increased by more than 40%. It was also becoming more difficult for the National Office to get detailed financial information and operating performance measures from the Branch Offices.

- For the first time in its history, the Better Way Foundation established and hired a staff of internal auditors. The National Office assigned an auditor to each

Branch Office. The new Group of seventy-four auditors reported directly to Charlie.

- Because the cost for the new Audit Group was higher than what Charlie anticipated, he directed that the Group's annual cost be charged back to the Branch Offices without any increase in Branch overhead budgets.

- In January of the final year of Charlie Yang's second employment agreement, the Better Way Foundation Board initiated an organization-wide Employee Attitude Survey. The Board of Directors' Management & Compensation Committee was required to conduct the survey. It was a part of the normal process for either extending or drafting a new employment agreement for the President and Chief Executive Officer position.

- The results of the survey were presented to the Board of Directors during a special meeting in May. Charlie was not invited to the meeting and he was not present.

- The Survey consultants presented the following Executive Summary of the recent findings:

  1. The morale throughout the organization is at the lowest level recorded during the five times this attitude survey has been conducted within the Better Way organization over the past twenty-one years.

  2. The top five responses listed as the potential causes for the drop in morale were:

     ✓ The lack of honest communications between the National Office and the Branch Directors.

     ✓ The lack of clear direction and support from the National Office.

     ✓ The lack of respect and appreciation of the work performed at the Branch level.

- ✓ The National Office's failure to keep key commitments made to the Branch Offices; and

- ✓ The loss of trust at all levels of the organization and in its leadership.

3. When asked, *"What would be the one change you would like to see in the organization at this time"*, 96% of the employee respondents said, *"a change in leadership at the top"*.

****

As the Chair of the Board's Management & Compensation Committee, I was tasked with developing the Board's approach to addressing the concerns expressed in the recent Employee Attitude Survey. I was also asked to meet with Charlie Yang, share with him the survey results and determine if the Better Way should express any interest in retaining Charlie's services as the Better Way President and CEO beyond his current agreement.

I met with Charlie two weeks later over a cup of coffee. He had a week to review his copy of the Employee Attitude Survey responses and the Executive Summary presented to the Board of Directors.

When Charlie entered the café, I could see the look of grave disappointment on his face. As soon as he sat down, he began to apologize for the direction that he had taken the organization. He agreed 100% that the buck stopped at his office.

In his words, *"I know that my miserable performance as the Better Way President over the last three years does not deserve an extension of the current or a new employment agreement."*

I could tell that he had lost all the confidence and trust he once had in his ability to lead the organization. Having held many senior leadership roles in large organizations during my career, instead of diving into what he did wrong, I spelled out the three things he had to do over the next six months to retain his job. They were:

1. First, you must regain the confidence and trust needed in yourself to continue in a senior leadership role.

2. Secondly, you must rebuild the trust within the Better Way organization back to the levels you found when you arrived, almost eight years ago; and

3. Lastly, you must make a presentation to the full Board of Directors during the December Board meeting. We all would like to hear at that time why you believe you should be retained as the Better Way President and CEO.

****

When Charlie entered the meeting room that evening in December, I don't believe any of the Board members felt he had any chance of retaining his job.

Charlie confidently opened his presentation by admitting to the Board that he had "masterfully screwed up" and should not have made major changes in the Better Way's leadership approach and operational strategy. In his words, *"I had convinced myself that the success I experienced during my first four years as the Better Way's President was all about me. I completely ignored the foundation that Mike Monahan had spent decades building to create this great organization."*

Charlie went on to provide the Board a recap of how he had spent the past six months. He had met for days with each Branch Director and their staff members. He admitted his "screw-up" to them and accepted all the blame. He also sincerely asked the Branch Directors for their candid and honest feedback.

95

In a remorseful voice, Charlie added, *"More importantly, for the first time I really listened. I made a commitment to involve all the Directors in a plan to right the wrongs—and it's a commitment I plan to keep. The goal will be to rebuild trust within the Better Way team and for us to return to being the strong organization we once were."*

Then, slowly Charlie walked over to the Board Chair and handed her a large envelope. Inside the envelope was a thick document. It was a ninety-five-page plan outlining the specific steps that he and his Branch Directors have agreed to take over the next twelve months to achieve the goal.

At the back of the document were the signatures of all seventy-four local Branch Directors.

****

Charlie and I met for dinner around the middle of January. We both had experienced delightful and enjoyable holiday seasons. We swapped stories about the holiday parties attended and the gifts we had received.

Although the 5 to 4 vote of approval by the Board of Directors was a *very close call*, Charlie also received a special gift earlier this month—a new five-year employment contract to continue as the Better Way's President and CEO.

I congratulated him for stepping up to the plate and doing what was "needed" to right the wrongs. Charlie smiled, and said, *"I could shoot myself for not seeing the writing on the wall four years ago."*

When I asked Charlie what he was suggesting, he quickly replied, *"I only needed to be like Mike"*

Questions to Ponder

1. How would you describe Charlie's situation?

2. In what ways can the lack trustworthiness make getting the most positive outcomes in most situations difficult?

3. Why did Charlie's approach to addressing too much travel and being too involved in the Branch offices ignore the broader issues of his situation?

4. When the Better Way Branch Directors asked for clarification on the new operational policies and procedures, Charlie failed to sometimes respond.

   How did this failure to consistently communicate contribute to worsening Charlie's situation?

5. What role do you think Charlie's "ownership of his mistakes" in not effectively managing the entire situation play in rebuilding confidence in his leadership?

6. When should Charlie have first recognized that he *"only needed to be like Mike"*?

7. If you in a situation where trust is lost, what can you do to re-establish mutual trust?

What are some of the lessons you should take away from this story and situation?

1. To effectively manage challenging situations, I will first work to ensure that I do what is required to gain and maintain the trust of others involved. Inspiring trust must be job one.

2.

3.

4.

5.

6.

7.

8.

CHAPTER TEN

I SHOULD HAVE KNOWN

It's hard to believe that I started this adventure eight years ago. In some ways it feels like yesterday. Yet, in other ways it feels like an eternity.

At least when I wake up in the mornings these days, I don't have to be concerned with leading an $800M privately held company and 1,200 employees while managing a debt of over $350M. Maybe now, I can also sleep at night and perhaps spend more time enhancing my decision-making skills.

How did a thirty-seven-year-old woman with two engineering degrees, a Ph.D. in Robotics and a name like Julie Juliet get herself in this somewhat agonizing position?

Well, an idea I had as a young girl is the primary culprit.

When I was about ten years old, I remember my dear grandmother requiring the help of a patient care assistant. I vividly recall one assistant who hurt her back multiple times performing tasks requiring physical exertion. I felt so sorry for her because I knew she was committed to properly taking care of my Grammie.

I said to myself at that time, *"there has to be a way to perform these tasks in a gentle and respectful yet safer manner."* I also thought, *"I wonder if I could someday invent and sell a robot or something to help with this important job."*

After I graduated from a private university in California with my Doctoral Degree, I spent three years obtaining research grants. The grant funding allowed me to act upon and think technically about my idea. I worked solo on an initial design of a robotic system that could be used to help patient care assistants in their effort to support bedridden patients in hospitals and long-term care facilities.

While visiting the new University Technology Incubator (UTI) that had just opened near my home, I met Joe, Jack and Johnny. They were leasing a small workplace in the UTI facility. I discovered that the three were working on several projects that utilized robotic controls. At first, they appeared to me to be standoffish and a little strange. However, as it turned out, they were just a group of entrepreneurial jocks with a couple of interesting patents.

After spending some time with them in their lab the next day, I realized that they were currently working on one project, which had technology similar to what I would need in my idea's design.

100

The synergy between the guys and me was amazing. Within weeks, we had come to an agreement to focus, as a team, on the robotic system I was designing and, as the old adage goes — the rest is history.

About a year later, Joe, Jack, Johnny and I formed a new startup company named Robotex. The following year, we won a contest sponsored by UTI and were awarded $1M of seed money to complete the development phase. Two years after that, we were able to raise our first round of venture capital funding. With those funds we were able to productionize a new robotic system we named "Robocare".

By that time, we were all working in a manner like the "Mod Squad". We jokingly called ourselves the "4Jays". We were working full time and putting in twelve-hour days. We feverishly finalized testing, manufacturing specifications and the packaging of the proprietary firmware. The firmware was the embedded software written to control and interface with the patented touch & lift sensor technology.

To make a long story short, two years later, we secured a third round of venture capital funding. With the third round, we expanded product and training program sales to hundreds of healthcare facilities. To our surprise, within a couple of years, Robotex's annual gross revenue had increased to over $800M.

Like most fast-growing technology startup companies, we were initially focused on capturing market share and not on profitability. With the rapid sales expansion, came significant production startup and marketing cost.

Consequently, part of my challenge at that point, as the now, President and CEO was to manage the heavy debt that Robotex was carrying on its balance sheet. I spent most of my time on the road convincing suppliers, investors and the financial markets that we had a vision of unlimited growth and would soon break even.

It was also my primary responsibility to pave the way for the upcoming Robotex Initial Public Offering (IPO). Based on the estimated initial stock price of $45 a share, by going public via an IPO, we anticipated raising over $875M and paying off most of the company's growing debt.

This was the start of me discovering that, even though I had significantly developed my executive leadership skills in many areas, I was missing a vital executive skill — *sound decision-making.*

It wasn't until a month after we had selected an underwriter and began the "Due Diligence and Filings" step of the five-step IPO process that my poor decision-making skills began to reveal themselves. As a result, everything we had worked so hard for over the past eight years began to unravel.

The first requirment needed for the underwriting process was to develop the Robotex financial "Registration Statement".

To make ensure that all the information provided in this key statement was accurate and without issues, the Robotex Board of Directors hired an independent investigation firm to review the backgrounds of all members of the Robotex senior management team. They were to also identify any legal problems faced by the company.

To everyone's surprise, after the investigation, the underwriter determined that there were three major issues. All the issues would present significant risk for Robotex in its effort to move forward with the IPO. The issues dated back to the start of the company and centered around me not properly vetting the backgrounds of and my relationships with the other "Jays".

****

Here is a summation of the three issues:

1. When I made the decision to team with Joe, Jack and Johnny eight years ago, I didn't keep in mind the first step in any sound decision-making process — which is "gather information and verify the facts". As it turns out, Joe, now Robotex's Chief Financial Officer and the "face" to our investment partners, was convicted of financial fraud  years ago. He had managed to successfully hide the conviction from everyone he now associates with. His deception included two legal name changes and multiple relocations.

I was so impressed with the apparent synergy between us, that I didn't do the necessary due diligence on the backgrounds of my three new acquaintances and future business partners.

2. When I reviewed the robotic patents that Jack, now Robotex's Chief Technology Officer, had been awarded when he was a young engineer, I missed the fact that he was just one of eight engineers on the patent application. This would prevent Robotex from using the patents in our design unless the other seven engineers could be found, and a mutual agreement was signed.

If I had known, I would have taken the second step in any sound decision-making process and would have identified all alternatives.

3. Johnny, now Robotex's Vice President and Director of Human Resources, had shared with me a few years ago that an ex-employee, as a part of a sexual harassment complaint, was suing Robotex. At the time, I was deeply involved in some critical robotic testing. Therefore, I made the decision to allow Johnny to handle the work associated with obtaining a private settlement of the incident and have it sealed. I did get a briefing on the $325,000 that Robotex had to pay to settle the compliant. However, I was never told that "Johnny" was the Robotex employee accused of the sexual harassment.

I was guilty of one of the most often-overlooked but important steps in the sound decision-making process — "thoughtfully reviewing all of your major decisions prior to pulling the trigger."

****

104

As I mentioned earlier, I am no longer with Robotex.

Because of the findings of the independent investigator, the Robotex IPO was never completed. Six months after I was forced to resign as the President and CEO and to leave the company, a competitor who simply assumed the company's debt acquired Robotex.

A few months after I was released as President and CEO of the now defunct Robotex, I was asked to be the guest speaker at a local business development meeting.

At first I was hesitant to do so. But later I decided to go ahead and accept their invitation and spoke to the group.

I finally determined that at some point I must surface and share my experiences and lessons learned. I am glad that I did. Because in retrospect, though painful, the Robotex adventure turned out to be a meaningful professional and personal growth opportunity for me.

In making decisions in both my professional and personal life these days, I am extremely careful to not "short-circuit" the decision-making process.

Never again do I want to be in the agonizing position of telling myself, *"I should have known"*.

Questions to Ponder

1. How would you describe Julie's situation?

2. In the world of data over-load, how did Julie Juliet, a smart person, become the unwitting victim of "ignorance."

3. What techniques can you use to ensure that you are using a systematic, reliable decision-making process to help manage challenging situations?

4. Julie blamed herself for her failure to "thoughtfully review all of her major decisions prior to pulling the trigger."

    As a leader of any situation, how do you determine which decisions should be considered major?

5. Julie assumed the outcomes gained through her technical and decision-making competencies would automatically equate to effectiveness in decision-making.

    What is the danger is this thinking?

6. What obstacles to effective decision-making have you observed in the most challenging situations you have been involved in?

What are some of the lessons you should take away from this story and situation?

1. In all challenging situations I face, I will be cognizant of the details associated with all major decisions I must make. I will make sure that I do not "short-circuit" the decision-making process.
2.
3.
4.
5.
6.
7.
8.

"Nothing can bring you happiness but yourself especially how you choose to think about your situation."

~ Ralph Waldo Emerson

Ralph Waldo Emerson, who went by his middle name Waldo, was an American essayist, lecturer, philosopher, and poet who led the transcendentalist movement of the mid-19th century.

ABOUT THE AUTHORS

Charlotte D. Grant-Cobb, PhD

Charlotte is a gifted author, change management coach and professional mentor. Dr. Grant-Cobb is an International Coaching Federation (ICF) Certified Coach.

Charlotte's extensive resume includes over 30 years of professional accomplishment. She had held senior leadership positions within Fortune 100 corporations, small business enterprises as well as in Federal and State government.

Charlotte earned her Bachelor of Science degree in Management and a Master of Business Administration degree from *Arizona State University*. She has also earned a professional Doctor of Philosophy in Nutrition Counseling degree from *LaSalle University*.

Charlotte uses her gifts to help her clients gain new awareness, create new habits, forge new pathways and embrace new experiences.

Ervin (Earl) Cobb

Earl is an accomplished corporate executive, leadership development coach, lecturer, and entrepreneur. He is currently the CEO & Managing Partner of Richer Life, LLC.

Earl has held senior technical and leadership positions within Fortune 100, Mid-market and Venture companies including *Honeywell, Inc.*, *Motorola, Inc.*, *The Reynolds and Reynolds Company* and *Wells Fargo Bank*. He is the former President, COO and CEO of the high-tech start-up, *MedContrax, Inc.*

Earl earned a Bachelor of Science degree in Electrical Engineering, with honors, from *Tennessee State University*. He graduated from *Arizona State University* with a Master of Science degree in Engineering.

Earl is a former Adjunct Professor of Management at the Keller Graduate School of Management of *DeVry University*. He has completed graduate studies at *Stanford University's Graduate School of Business, the Sloan School of Management at MIT* and the *Center for Creative Leadership*.

CPSIA information can be obtained
at www.ICGtesting.com
Printed in the USA
LVHW052208270121
677519LV00010B/294